Threads of Two Voices

The Paths of An Artist and a Poet Entwine to Create an Exquisitely Beautiful Message

by:
Janet Purcell
and
John C. Campbell

Cover art by Lisa Rothamel

Balboa Press books may be ordered through booksellers or by contacting:

Balboa Press
A Division of Hay House
1663 Liberty Drive
Bloomington, IN 47403
www.balboapress.com
1-(877) 407-4847

ISBN: 978-1-4525-4527-1 (sc)
ISBN: 978-1-4525-4528-8 (e)

Library of Congress Control Number: 2012900784

Printed in the United States of America

Balboa Press rev. date: 04/10/2012

BALBOA.
PRESS
A DIVISION OF HAY HOUSE

Special Message

" This message from Spirit is brought to you with divine love and gratitude."

At the time of final proofing of this book selected passages were emphasized in a vision to Janet. They are referenced below. The passages provided by Spirit have been italicized within the body of the spiritual metaphors, as well. The passages and coinciding art work are meant to provide a blueprint for living a balanced life. These images and messages will have global impact beyond the experience of the reader.

Seeds Of Time
The time is now to understand the global impact of humanities choices.

Souls Yearning
The yearning to return home is the soul's remembrance of the "spark of life."

Knowing
The intuitive connection to "one's heart" is the ability to connect with God.

Living
The book is a blueprint for "healthful living" to achieve a balanced life.

INTRODUCTION

Two ordinary individuals on separate spiritual paths share their insights each in their own unique way. "Threads of Two Voices" could easily be two separate books and yet combining them into one teaches us how two seemingly different expressions can actually be a common story. Janet Purcell a writer, shares her insights with words, while John Campbell, an artist, shares his insights with pictures. John's pictures (Spiritual Abstractions) have been arranged in order of his choosing as Janet's poetry (Spiritual Metaphors) has been arranged in the order of her choosing, then interlaced, showing one opposite the other. Now it is for you, the reader to discover the relationships and underlying message.

Both visionaries believe that to fully appreciate what art and poetry offer, one must see beyond what is actually there. This means seeing with your inner eye and hearing with your heart's ear. It means opening your spirit to the message that lies within each series of words and each collage of color. To do this, the reader must take time, find solitude and reflect on the deep meaning that the stimulants in this book provide. The words are not necessarily related to the art, it will be up to the reader to feel either a connection or a separation.

To fully experience this material, the authors suggest that the book can be read in several ways. On the first reading, you may choose to only view the art. For the second time through, you may read the poetry. When you pick up the book for a third time, you'll be ready to ask yourself questions about the two voices. How are they the same? Different? How do they resonate with your own 'voice' or feelings?

After an interval of time, look though the book again and see if you can find words for the pictures and pictures for the words. See if the expressions feel different to you now. Is it more familiar or is there some discord? Explore these feelings and see where they take you and what new threads of insight you receive.

When you learn to listen to your own voice, you are empowered to live in harmony with yourself. It is through this path of self-discovery that divine love evolves, leading you to the light.

Acknowledgements

Writing is always a collaborative effort. Many people have contributed to the evolution of this book in various ways. We have had many teachers: those who have blessed our lives with their presence, and those who have presented us with challenges, resulting in changes in perspective and our spiritual growth. We are grateful to all of our teachers.

It is in this spirit that we both wish to give our heartfelt thanks to all those who have contributed to our growth and this book. It is our prayer that this book is worthy of their teachings.

We wish to give special thanks to Lisa Rothamel for her tireless hours of effort in laying out the spiritual metaphors in this book and for placing the spirit guide images interlaced throughout the spiritual metaphors. We also wish to give special thanks to Mary Holden for her editing, enthusiastic support and guidance. Mary can be contacted at her website www.marylholdeneditor.com.

Your energy is always a light beam
in an often gray and dark world.
I am greatful to have you as a friend

Be Peace
John
Campbell

🐾 Sparkey & Caroline
say Hi !

Listen to your heart!
Rev. Joseph Purcell

Possibilities

Journeying inward sets in motion

the birthing of limitless possibilities,

to be carried on waves of healing.

Often breaking on enlightenment barriers,

journeying on to the distant shores of home.

Creator in Creation

Self

The healing of one's soul
is based upon the preponderances
of the meaning of "Self."

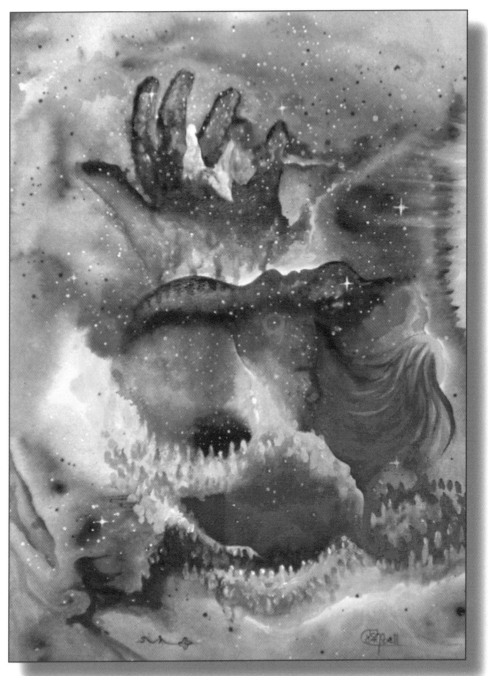

Cosmic Conversation

Clarity

The cadence of inner peace

is marked by the drumming for clarity

of one's purpose for living.

The Guardian

Journey

Discernment of truth

is rooted in the embodiment

of the soul's journey upon the earth.

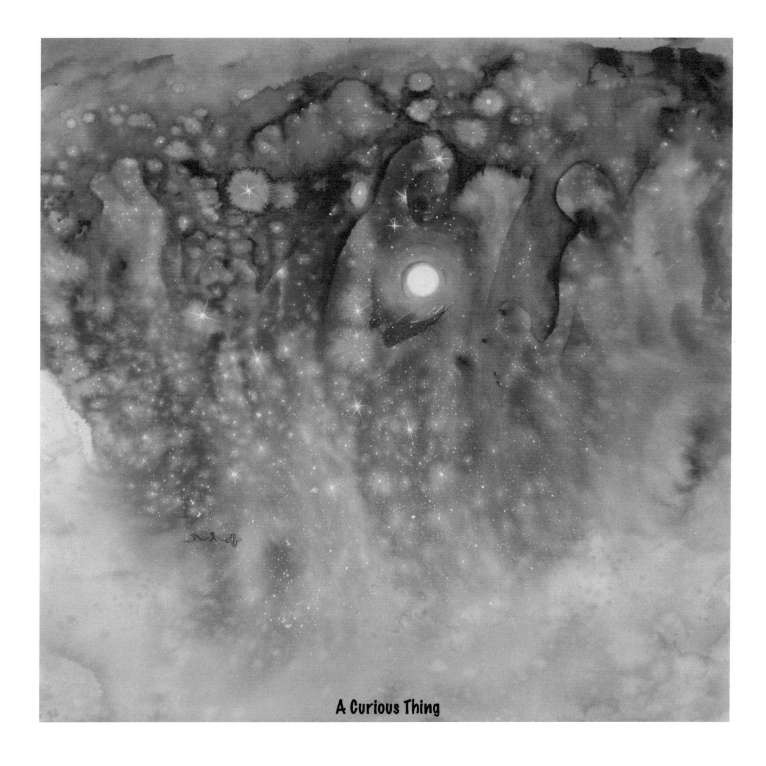

A Curious Thing

Contentment

The air of contentment washes over us

when the foundation floods with

remembrances of who

we are, and rises within us

into the soundings of

heaven and earth rejoicing

and giving thanks!

Passing the Orb

Gratitude

For this moment you must give thanks

for who you were,

who you are,

and for who you shall become:

one aspect of Self.

Mystic Orb

Choices

On heaven and earth all is quiet,

listening to the voices decrying the absence of peace,

a breach of peace,

born out of one's own choices.

The breaching of peace can only

be summed up with one phrase:

absence of love.

Maker of Worlds

Sharing

The pain that is borne on the shoulders of one

must be shared with another to still the cries of fear.

Fear strikes deep into the hearts of many,

yet one's reflecting quietly can bring stillness

and peace once more into the heart.

The Seeding

T
R
U
T
H

Worry not for thou will indeed inherit the earth.

From the ashes you will rise up to meet the heavens

with greatness like no other has seen.

The search for truth has brought this to you,

rejoice and give thanks!

Guardian of the Egg

Forgiveness

A forgiving heart beats with peace,

and joy becomes the ripples in the pond.

The more you forgive yourself

the larger the ripples become,

finally reaching those you love and

those whom you have yet to love.

Inspiration

 # Reaching Out

Kindness is a condition of the heart.

The heart reaches out to another,

feels the pain and sadness

stirring in their soul.

The stirring reaches out and connects to another,

releasing acts of kindness.

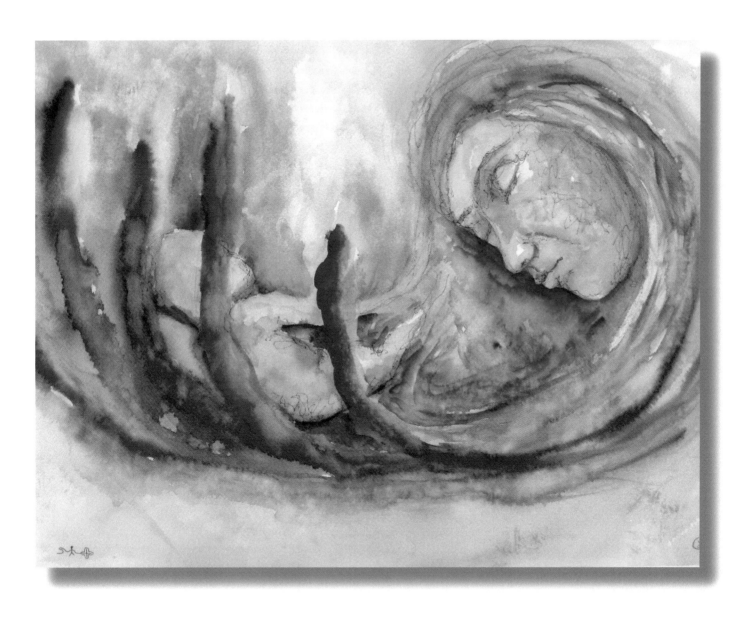

Life's Journey

Lost

When distress creeps

into tomorrow,

one must reach deeply

into yesterday

to find that

which was lost.

Cosmic Birthing

Sunrise

Your doubts are based upon the morrows.

The dawning of a new sunrise

brings with it the possibility of change,

and new choices before the sun sets.

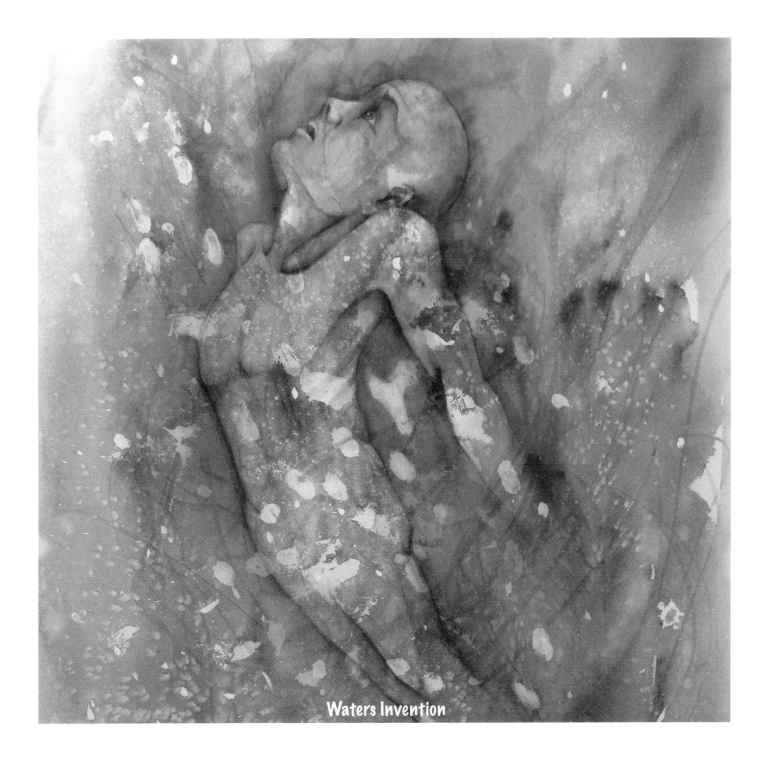
Waters Invention

Connection

Uncertainties of the unknown

is the soul crying out for connection –

connection to Creator of All,

a power far greater than our own.

Learning to let go and trust in the Power

relieves us from concerns that are trite.

Only sourcing the Power from within

can bring us peace.

Cry out no more

knowing that you are connected!

Natures Birth

Harmony

Integrity is the feeling one has when

the song of the heart sings in tune.

When you are not in tune,

look at the discord in your life.

Synchronize the tune and

harmony will again reign.

Fairy in the Garden

Angels of Peace

With trumpets blowing,

the angels are heralding their rumors of peace,

proclaiming the peace ringing out.

Peace has never been far from sight,

only hidden from the visionless.

Join the procession of angels

leading the multitudes,

for the peace you carry in your hearts

is the trumpets that are blowing!

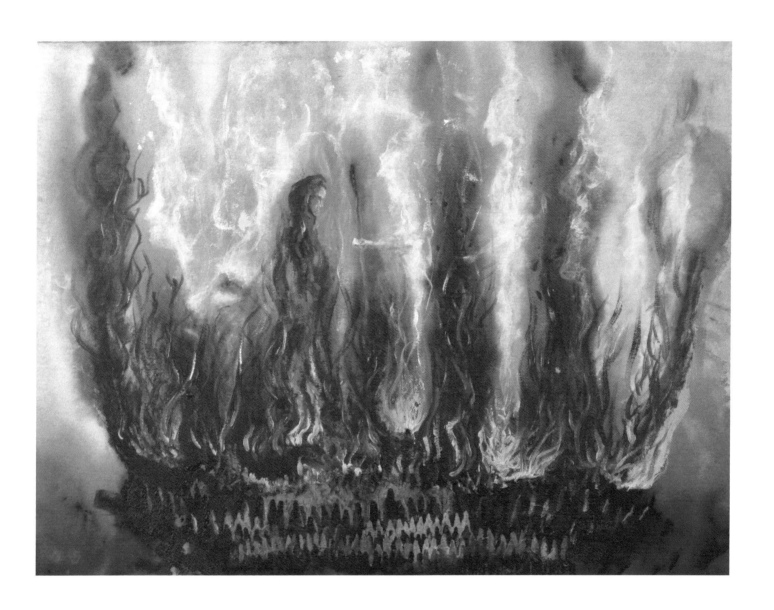

Smoke Talker

Home

Welcoming home is of the heart,
the heart yearning to be free of all the
entanglements of our earthbound existence.

Welcome home, my dear one,
you are loved beyond measure.
For the light that shines deep inside of you
shines brightly upon the realms of the heavenly
"The light of love"

Welcome home,
for know that within you "is home."
The light within you is the light
that reaches out and touches
all that is...ONE!
Welcome Home...

Convergence

Trust

The light cometh when it is needed.

Lift up your heart and let the angels sing.

Trust comes from "knowing"

that all creatures big and small

must learn to trust.

For within trust comes the love

that is revealed to all.

Trust my dear one, for you are

a child of Creator.

Trust my dear one,

for you are loved immeasurably.

Trust my dear one,

for all who trust shall know LOVE!

Sisters Adrift

 # Touching

When one loses focus

    and all around life is swirling,

        reach out with compassion and

            touch the life of another.

For it is with the touching of another

    that you will find your liberation.

        The loss of focus is but a reflection

            of the soul's momentary hesitation,

                while waiting for the journey

                to become clear.

The direction of the journey will bring clarity

    when one reaches out to comfort another!

    Two souls comforting together

        carries us into all that is ...Love.

Sweet Dreams

A  Multifaceted Soul

Imperfections of the soul
integrated with cracks and fractures
reveals the crevasses
inherent within the jewel.
Amalgamation of life experiences
serves as a catalyst.
Melding together of the fractures and cracks
gives way to the final restoration.
A completeness of the soul's fundamental nature
a multifaceted jewel
softly shimmering and vibrating
Perfectly created!

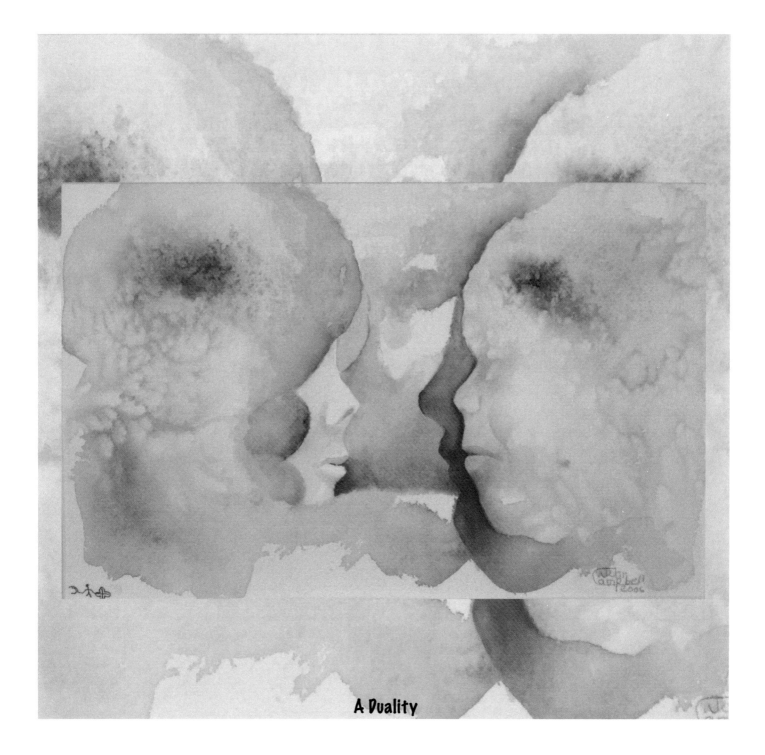

A Duality

Threads

The truth of who you are

is embossed in the threads

that make up the cover

with which you seek solace!

Consoling

Friendship

Friendship is like a river
that runs between two shores.
The waters that touch both shores
are but a fraction of the depth
that flows between.
The ebbs and flows are ever changing,
as is the friendship that runs alongside,
the joining of friendship together
is a common current that runs between.

Respect, joy, understanding and concern,
knowing that the river is ever shifting,
affected by droughts and storms,
ever eroding the shore.

Place one grain of sand upon the banks.
When the storms come,
so shall the weathering of the shores endure.

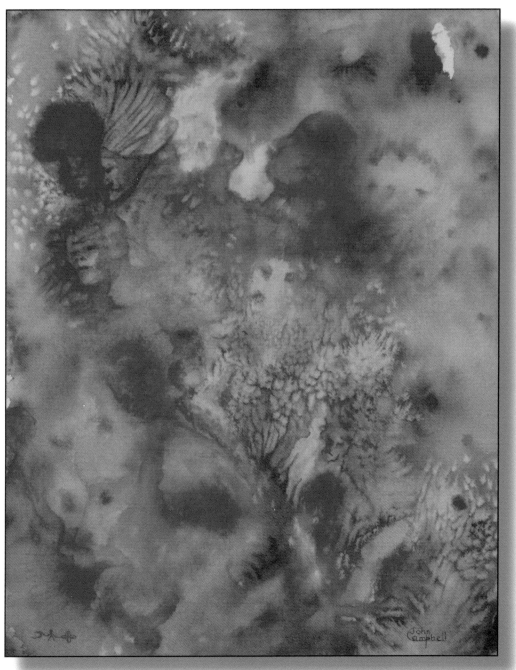

Face It

Beggar

Where does the beggar be,

for he has no home, no family, no friends

and no place to be.

What make ye a beggar be?

His reply: "For the burning in my heart,

for the answers I cannot find,

a beggar I will be!"

Bringing Forth

Time

It is in a moment's time, the day after.

Time eludes me, for there is no time,
only teardrops of the moment.
As the sun rises
so are the teardrops dried
and another yesterday has been created.
In this instant let all the yesterdays
break way into the holograph of life,
only to
return again and again ...
to wholeness.

Reaching for Humanity

Life

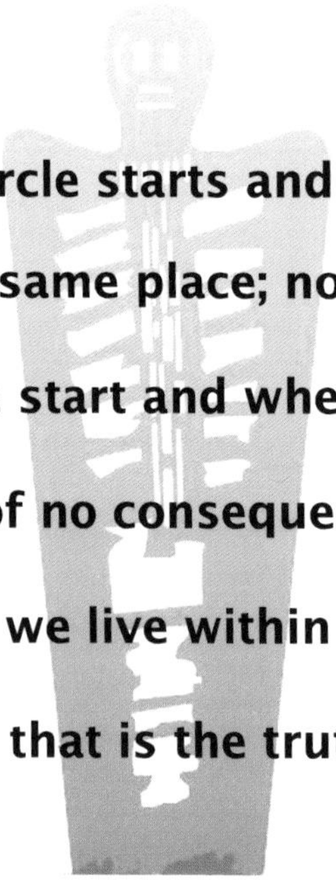

A circle starts and ends

in the same place; nowhere.

Where we start and where we end

is of no consequence;

it is how we live within the circle

– that is the truth!

Journey to Innocence

Seeds of Time

Sowing the seeds of "time"
the relentlessness of time
stirring desire, self-imposed boundaries,
self-denial, future hope, past times,
present time...in the moment.
The tender feelings, hope, desires, promises,
broken promises, loves, death, departure, finality,
and rebirth still the unsown seeds of time have
yet to take root.

Tomorrow is today!
The seeds of time wait for no person.
Lingering momentarily, the seeds of time wait to
be honored, cherished, cultivated, and
nurtured with love, like the tenderness
of first love.

Wait no longer, sow your seeds
realize that this is all.
All that can be is wrapped up
in the sown seeds of time.

Plant, nurture, cultivate and harvest – the time is **NOW**,
for home is just a second away...regrets exist forever!

Devotion

Listen

Listen, listen

for that which you hear

will be amplified a thousand times over.

Be silent, feel – hear your silence;

it is the space you must travel to,

what you yearn for.

 Self can only be found by listening.

As you move across your silence into your heart,

feel the nectar of sweetened quiet,

you are ONE with all that is…Self!

The Student

Soul's Yearning

Our soundings and rumblings come from the depths of despair of the soul; the immortal cry to be set free, resounding into the wailings and screams for remembrance, the hearts yearning to return home.

Home resides in the omnipresent light that casts a shadow from afar. Our soul's yearning is set on fire with the plethora of passions for the freedom, once kindred to the soul's spark of life.

Do not despair for within your grasp,
you need only to
reach out and touch another to still the soul's
cries, for we are all One – you are home!

The Bird

The Measure of
a Human

The measure of a human
is not how we believe,
it is how we live.
Listening to one's own heart
gives us the unlimited pools of
possibilities to draw from.
Those same unlimited possibilities
provide the framework of a
Spirit living within a human environment.
Our lives are like a greenhouse, and
it affects the growth and maturity
of the human spirit.
Choosing a possibility from the pools of the unlimited
sets in motion the seeding, germination
and the springing forth of life –
the completeness of a human spirit.

Enlighten

Divine Revelation

One's intuition reflects the inner knowledge

Our Essence

The essence is the caretaker of divine revelation

The Mystery

Knowing

The filling of one's heart

comes from the wonder of "knowing."

Connecting to our Creator becomes clear.

Just as each moment is spent

so are the past and the future.

Sourcing one's self

is the ability to connect with God.

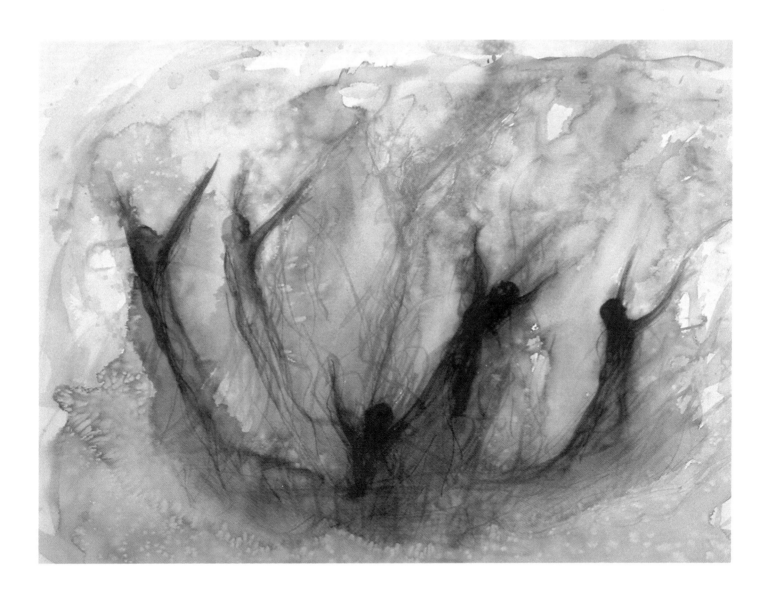

Emergence Rejoice

Dependence

After feeling your fear
you must bring it forward
into the tomorrows.
Remembering
that one's life of dependence
is based upon this fear.

The Instruction

Living

The coming upon the earth

for a short or long time

is not dependent upon the longevity of health,

but on healthful living.

The Giving

The Package

Judge not the package

lest the package unravels.

Orb Carrier

Wholeness

The unsettledness that dwells deep in one's Soul

is the concern that one will not be whole.

The wholeness that one yearns for

is found in the faith that all is as it should be.

One's yearning sets in motion

the quest for inner peace.

The peace we seek is at our fingertips.

Reaching inward connects us to our peace.

The connection to wholeness of SELF!

The Watchers

Vessel

The pouring out of love from the vessel,

caring for another human being – a stranger,

egoless, the soul overflowing with caring,

brings strangers' souls together.

And yet, not quite strangers,

echoes of a soul caring for another –

a new arrival

abundantly flowing, multiplying many times over,

the refilling of the vessel

egoless, touching another stranger –

yet... not a stranger.

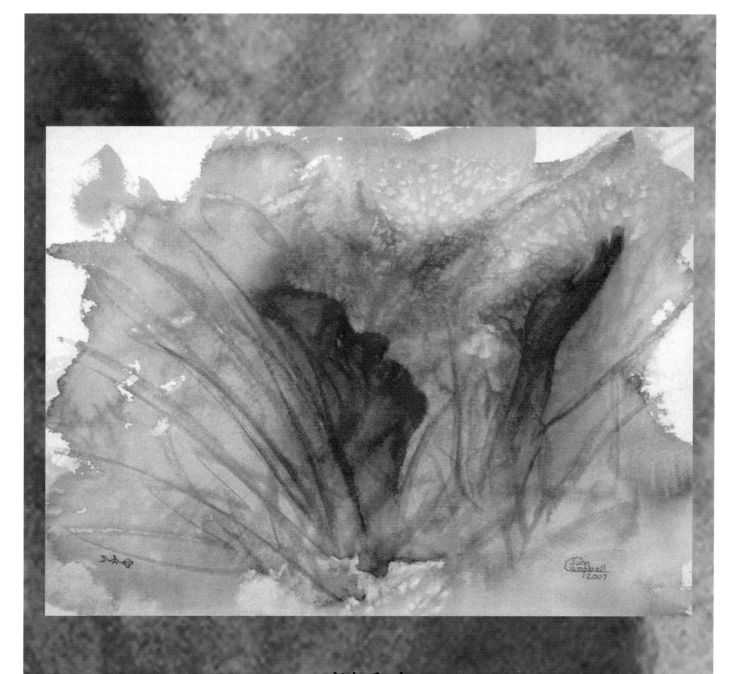

Light Touch

ABOUT JOHN CAMPBELL
and his Spiritual Abstractions

"If you can picture it you can achieve it."

John C. Campbell considers himself an emerging artist--emerging from over 33 years in a career as a software engineer. His interest in art goes back to early childhood. The family story is that he was drawing before he could speak. He believed that natural talent was all that was needed and painted for his own pleasure. Believing the myth that artists cannot be self-supporting, he began a career in computer technology back when very few people knew what a computer was. In his mid-twenties he was so entangled with the struggles of life that he stopped painting. By his mid-thirties he had destroyed all his works and threw away all his painting tools.

It wasn't until the late 1990s that John gradually returned to his first love-- art. He took classes and worked with various established artists, learning techniques. He became proficient, but the results were not satisfying to him because he felt that they lacked both energy and expression.

Around that same time John also studied alternative healing modalities. He learned massage, sand box therapy and dream interpretation, chakra healing, DNA energetic healing, light body work and several other energy healing techniques. Additionally he became a ReiKi Master/Teacher. This path brought him back in touch with his energetic self which he now expresses in his paintings.

One day, while working with one of his energy teachers, John understood that his true healing qualities were the marriage of both art and energy work. In his next painting he let go of the techniques he'd learned and just painted without a preconceived ending in mind. When the painting was done he knew this was his path.

John Campbell met Janet Purcell when he was a student in the ReiKi class she taught. When Janet first approached him about this book he was cool to the idea. He had his own plans for a book of art but was stuck in the 'I'm too busy' state of mind. Plus he was putting together a web art gallery, painting, working a day job and taking care of things at home. Then there was the whole issue of his pictures and Janet's words. He couldn't see how words he had not written could be related to his art.

In his meditations he was encouraged to open up to the idea. He heard two voices speaking different words but saying the same thing. And then saw this book as a way of demonstrating how a common view can be expressed very differently and perhaps the book might demonstrate the value of listening.

With this book John hopes the reader learns that in a universe of infinite possibilities no one viewpoint can be complete. No one perspective can be the only true view. All views have truth in them, and all views are incomplete.

The paintings by John are of a genre he calls spiritual abstraction. "Spiritual" because of how they arrive, and because they bring a message that gives him insights and great comfort. He adds the name "abstractions" because they are a two-dimensional visual representation of his five dimensional experiences, so they can only be at best an abstract representation. As the reader mediates on his paintings, a sense of their dimensional depth will be revealed.

When John paints a spiritual abstraction, he does not have a preconceived idea of the subject. He does no sketches or studies nor does he have any ideas of a completed painting in mind. He sets up a canvas clears his mind and enters a state of meditation then at some point he is moved to apply paint, typically a process of splashing and moving it around with out thought. When the energy leaves, he sets the painting aside to dry. Later he comes back and studies it to see what images are suggested.

Often the image is clear but sometimes it is not apparent. In either case, once he feels it is time, he adds more paint. After a while the image may develop to the point where it is clear and then he applies the rules of design and composition to complete the work. Once the technical work is complete he mediates to hear a name and then he signs it.

The paintings in this book are arranged in an order to tell an overall story of spiritual birth, life and rebirth. This is a simple yet complicated story so the viewer will discover sub-plots occurring with in the relationships of two or three paintings, and then of course each painting is a story within itself.

Reading paintings is an art that has been in decline since the advent of the printing press and public reading education. Visual images can and do have very powerful impacts on us especially if we are not familiar with how to read such images.

So how does one read a painting? There are many different ways. Some approaches are culturally dependent, some are experience dependent, some art is special-knowledge dependent, all are environmentally dependent, and a few are open ended and meant to challenge common assumptions.

Spiritual abstractions fall into the last category--they are meant to challenge common assumptions with grace and ease. These painting are not typically meant to be an in-your-face challenge. They are made attractive to the eye with color and motion that draw your attention and gently ask questions.

The key to studying spiritual abstractions is to make observations then ask questions. Search inside yourself for answers. When an answer comes, again observe the painting see how it feels. Regardless of the feeling, challenge the answer with your life experiences. Does the answer fit? If not, why not? Ask if there is a different answer to the question, or perhaps a different question.

All of this dialogue is part of what John calls the cosmic conversation. It is through this conversation that we begin to awake from sleepwalking and grow into awareness. It is only through awareness that humans can walk through the veil of deception to enlightenment.

John creates works of art that come through him, not of him. They are a source of insight and energetic healing for others to draw upon. It is John's prayer that you find insight and comfort in his works and he hopes that they might act as aids on your life's journey.

You can reach John via his web art gallery at www.JohnCampbellArtS.com.

ABOUT JANET PURCELL
and her Sacred Metaphors

"A Journey of a Thousand Miles Begins with a Single Step –Lao Tsu"

Janet Purcell grew up in a small farming community in Nebraska. The only child of a farmer and a schoolteacher, Janet was accustomed to listening to the sound of the corn growing and the company of earthworms as they crawled through freshly tilled soil, seeking protection.

Her deep passion for empowering and helping others comes from these roots, as well as from her recent experiences. Desperately worried about the ill health of her parents, on the way to work one day she uttered a prayer, "I am at a crossroads in my life. I need some help!" Within weeks Janet heard a voice, telling her to quit her government job, even though she was just short of retirement. With a leap of faith, uncertain what Spirit had in store for her, she listened, and heeded the divine message. She began a spiritual journey--one that changed her life forever.

She discovered that a gift for writing sacred metaphors became present in her life when she was searching for answers or direction. Janet is aware of several spirit guides and was informed by them to recognize and differentiate between the words *intuition, revelation* and *discernment.* In meditation, she became unsure of what these words meant. She asked friends and colleagues for help, which added even more confusion.

After a week of searching, she woke up one morning and was inspired to take up pen and paper and write words she heard. They were coming too fast. She couldn't keep up until she went to a computer keyboard and typed as fast as the dictation was flowing. The result of this listening and typing became the sacred metaphors in this book.

Janet says, "The purpose of these metaphors is to transform and awaken you. They are to help bring about changes in your life through understanding, compassion and clarity. She believes they will help you become more intuitive so that you can begin to better understand yourself and others. Her sincere wish for you is that your interpretation for each of these sacred metaphors will bring you a deeper understanding of yourself and spark your own personal search for joy, peace and love in your heart!"

Currently she has a clinical practice, integrating life coaching and energy medicine, as well as providing spiritual counseling. She teaches classes on self-healing, using Reiki, Healing Touch and Quantum Touch protocols. Janet leads retreats to sacred sites throughout the Southwest. She has been an active member of the Phoenix chapter of Compassion in Action, dedicated to providing a loving and supportive presence to the dying and their families. Janet is also an Interfaith Minister, ordained in 2007.

A task given to her by Spirit, and now a passion, was to create a not-for-profit organization, Desert Spirit Pueblo Retreat Center. Her vision for this retreat center is to minister to those recovering from life threatening illness. This project is in the formative stage.

The mother of three children, Janet lives in Phoenix with her eccentric roommate, a dachshund named Barnie.

Janet may be reached via email healingnrg3@cox.net
or her website at www.Spiritual-Matters.com.

Meditation on the Images

Meditation on the Words

Meditation on the Words and Images together

CPSIA information can be obtained
at www.ICGtesting.com
Printed in the USA
LVIW010027080512

280774LV00001B